Creepy Crawlers

Lynn Huggins-Cooper

QEB

QEB Publishing

Copyright © QEB Publishing 2008

Published in the United States by
QEB Publishing, Inc.
3 Wrigley, Suite A
Irvine, CA 92618

www.qed-publishing.co.uk

Library of Congress Control Number: 2008011767

ISBN 978 1 59566 847 9

Author: Lynn Huggins-Cooper
Edited, designed, and picture researched by:
  Starry Dog Books Ltd.
Consultant: Sally Morgan

Printed in China

Picture credits
Key: t = top, b = bottom, l = left, r = right, c = center.
FC = front cover, BC = back cover.

A = Alamy, BSP = Big Stock Photo.com, C = Corbis,
D = Dreamstime.com, G = Getty Images, ISP = iStockphoto.com,
PL = Photolibrary, PS = Photoshot, S = Shutterstock.com,
SDB = Starry Dog Books, SPL = Science Photo Library.

1 D/ © Fishguy66; 2–3 S/ © Julie Scholz; 4t S/ © Graham
Prentice, 4b C/ © Layne Kennedy; 5 S/ © Dmitrijs
Mihejevs; 6t PL/ © Patti Murray, 6b ISP/ © John Pitcher;
7 BSP/ © Katherine Haluska; 8t BSP/ © Stuart Elflett, 8b
D/ © Pixelman; 9 D/ © Fishguy66; 10t A/ © Holt Studios
International Ltd, 10b © Christian Fuchs; 11 PL/ © Oxford
Scientific; 12b PL/ © Densey Clyne/Oxford Scientific, 12–13
ISP/ © Jeridu; 13 BSP/ © Styve Reineck; 14t C/ © B. Borrell
Casals; Frank Lane Picture Agency, 14b A/ © Bjorn Holland;
15 D/ © Musat; 16bl A/ © Florian Schulz, 16–17 BSP/ ©
Michal Boubin; 17br A/ © WildPictures; 18 D/ © Fouroaks;
19t A/ © Leslie Garland Picture Library, 19b S/ © Jorge Pedro
Barradas de Casais; 20t A/ © Holt Studios International
Ltd, 20b PL/ © Konrad Wothe/Oxford Scientific; 21 S/ ©
Dmitrijs Mihejevs; 22t D/ © Pufferfishy, 22b D/ © Xenobug;
23 C/ © DK Limited; 24t C/ © David A. Northcott, 24b A/ ©
Maximilian Weinzierl; 25 A/ © blickwinkel; 26t PS/ © George
Bernard, 26b PL/ © Paulo De Oliveira/Oxford Scientific; 27
SPL/ © Eye of Science; 28 (all pics) SDB/ © Nick Leggett; 29
SDB/ © Nick Leggett.

Contents

Watch out!

From tropical **rain forests** to dry deserts, from meadows and parks to our own homes, creepy crawlers are everywhere—so watch out!

▲ *Weta are large, wingless crickets that live in New Zealand and on the nearby islands.*

Different types

Very many of the creepy crawlers we see around us are insects. All insects, such as dragonflies, beetles, wasps, and ants, have six legs and three body parts. There are over a million different **species** of insects crawling, flying and creeping across the Earth. Other creepy crawlers include spiders and, in the oceans, **crustaceans** such as crabs and shrimps.

Creepy?

Although many people are scared of insects and other creepy crawlers, they really are amazing creatures worth taking a closer look at. They can survive in the most hostile environments, including places that people cannot live.

◄ *Scientists believe that over 90 per cent of all the creatures alive today are insects.*

Large ancestors

Some creepy crawlers are huge. The Malaysian giant stick insect, for example, grows about as long as a man's arm, and goliath beetles can weigh as much as a family-sized bar of chocolate. But today's creepy crawlers are small compared to creatures from **prehistoric** times. Some 390 million years ago, 8-feet-long sea scorpions swam in the oceans and 10-feet-long centipedes scurried through the forests.

▼ Goliath beetles are probably the largest, heaviest insects in the world. They help keep the Earth clean by eating dead plant material.

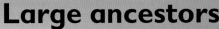

Spooky spiders

Spiders are scary to millions of people, perhaps because they can scuttle so fast. Some spiders leap out and ambush their victims. Others inject poison when they bite.

▲ *A funnel web spider sits at the entrance to its burrow, ready to pounce on its* **prey***.*

Tarantulas

There are an incredible 800 to 1000 species of tarantulas living in warm parts of the world, such as Africa, southern Europe, Australia, South America, and Asia. Some live in deserts, others prefer rain forests. They eat insects, other spiders, small **reptiles**, frogs, and even small birds.

Funnel web spiders

Funnel web spiders live in Australia. They have sharp, strong **fangs** that they use to inject **venom** into their prey, which includes beetles and skinks. Their venomous bites can cause serious illness or death in humans, but cats and dogs are more resistant to the poison.

◄ *Although tarantulas are venomous, no one is known to have died as a result of a tarantula bite.*

▼ *The female golden orb web spider strings her webs between trees. The webs are strong enough to snare birds, although the birds are not eaten by the spider.*

Golden orb web spiders

Golden orb web spiders live in Africa and Australia. The spiders are small, but their webs can be up to 6.5 feet wide, and can last for several years. The silk is so strong that it has been used in the South Pacific to make fishing nets. Some people have used the webs to cover wounds and stop them bleeding.

Foul fact!

"Golden" in the golden orb web spider's name describes the color of the web, rather than the spider itself.

Foul flies

Flies can be very annoying, buzzing around our heads and landing on our food. If, however, you take a closer look, you will see that they are truly amazing flyers.

▶ *Blowflies include greenbottles and bluebottles. They are easily recognized by their metallic sheen.*

Snakeflies

There are about 200 different snakefly species. Snakeflies live in North America, Europe, and central Asia. They eat small prey, such as aphids and young caterpillars. The female lays her eggs under bark. The eggs hatch into **larvae** that live under bark and in **leaf litter**.

▼ *An adult snakefly can lift its head high above the rest of its body, in a similar way to an attacking snake.*

Blowflies

Female blowflies lay eggs on meat or on the open wounds of injured animals, such as sheep. A female blowfly can lay up to 2000 eggs in her lifetime. Only eight hours after being laid, the eggs hatch into maggots, which feed on the meat.

Foul fact!

Snakeflies are one of only two groups of insects that can run backward at full speed.

Robber flies

Robber flies are often found in dry, sandy places. They are aggressive hunters, preying on spiders, beetles, other flies, butterflies, bees, and other flying insects. A robber fly catches its prey in the air. It has a sharp point on its head that it uses to pierce the flesh of its prey. Then it injects **saliva** into the other creature. The saliva paralyzes the prey, so that the robber fly can suck out its juices.

▶ *A robber fly has a thick, bristly moustache that helps to protect its face from prey struggling to escape.*

Putrid parasites

Parasites are creatures that live by feeding off another living creature, called the host. They are among the creepiest of creepy crawlers.

▼ *The* **eyestalks** *of this snail are infected with parasitic flatworms. The flatworms wriggle inside the eyestalks, and look to a bird like tasty caterpillars.*

▲ *An aphid parasite searches for aphids using the long* **antennae** *on its head.*

Aphid parasites

Aphid parasites are tiny black wasps. An adult lays its egg inside an aphid. The egg hatches and the parasite develops into an adult wasp inside the aphid's body. The wasp leaves its host by cutting a circular hole in the aphid and flying out.

Parasitic flatworms

One species of parasitic flatworm preys on birds. It starts life as an egg, found in a bird's droppings. A snail slithers along and eats the bird's droppings, including the flatworm's egg. The egg hatches into a flatworm inside the snail. The flatworm moves through the snail, and settles in one of its eyestalks. A bird eats the snail, and the flatworm ends up inside the bird's stomach, where it lays its eggs. The flatworm's eggs pass out in the bird's droppings, and the cycle begins again.

Ichneumon wasps

There are thousands of species of ichneumon wasps. Females have a long tube, called an ovipositor, at the end of their body, which they use to inject their eggs into other animals. Some species inject their eggs into caterpillars. When the eggs hatch into larvae, the caterpillars split open and die.

◀ *Some species of ichneumon wasps lay their eggs under tree bark close to wood wasp larvae that are living in the wood. They lay their eggs in tunnels made by the larvae.*

Bulgy bodies

Some creepy crawlies have large, bulging bodies. The body of a queen termite is so big she can hardly move.

Hercules moth caterpillar

The caterpillar of the Hercules moth lives in the rain forests of Australia. It is named after the ancient Greek hero Hercules. According to legend, he was the strongest man in the world. The caterpillar turns into one of the world's largest moths. An adult Hercules moth has a wingspan of up to 12 inches, making it about the size of a dinner plate.

Termites

Termites have lived on Earth for an amazing 200 million years. There are more than 2500 species. Termites live in **colonies** made up of one or several large, egg-laying queens and thousands, or even millions, of much smaller **worker** and **soldier** termites. The queen termite can lay up to 86,000 eggs in one day.

Foul fact!

The female Hercules moth has no mouth for feeding. All she does before she dies is mate and lay eggs.

◀ *The Hercules moth caterpillar has a large, squishy body covered in yellow spikes. It feeds on the leaves of the bleeding heart tree.*

▲ *After mating, a queen termite loses her wings and she starts a new colony. The head and legs of this queen are visible on the left.*

Termite mounds

Termites build huge nests. Some species build them as tall, clay mounds. Others build them in tree bases and underground. In the forest, termites have a useful job as "garbage removers." They chew up dead wood, making it decay quickly. This makes the soil rich and a good place for plants to grow. In towns, termites can be a pest, as they chew up the wood in houses. In the United States, termites cause more damage to property than storms and fires combined.

▶ *Termite mounds on the African grasslands generally range from about 3 to 10 feet tall. Many of them are about the height of an adult man.*

Loathsome legs

Spiders are not the only creepy crawlies with scary legs. The massive Japanese spider crab has ten legs, at least as long as a tall man!

Japanese spider crab

The Japanese spider crab lives in the Pacific Ocean around Japan. Using its two front legs, which are specialized for feeding, it eats mainly dead animals and shellfish that it finds on the seabed. It is preyed on by even bigger octopuses and by fishermen.

▲ *Scolopendra centipedes grasp their prey with the claws on the ends of their powerful legs.*

Scolopendra centipedes

Scolopendra centipedes can be more than 12 inches long—longer than a school ruler. Most scolopendra centipedes are **nocturnal**. They hunt at night for insects and mice.

Using a pair of poison claws directly under the head, they bite their prey again and again, injecting it with venom. The bite of a scolopendra centipede can be very painful to a human.

◀ *The Japanese spider crab has a legspan about as long as a small car.*

▼ The basic structure of a harvestman has not changed much in 400 million years.

Harvestmen

Harvestmen belong to a big family—there are more than 6400 species worldwide. They eat flies, mites, small slugs, spiders, decaying plants, **fungi**, and bird droppings. After each meal, the harvestman pulls each of its eight legs through its jaws, one at a time, to clean them. If a harvestman is attacked by a bird, it releases a terrible stink as a defense.

Foul fact!

If a harvestman is attacked and loses a leg, the leg continues to twitch. The predator is distracted and the harvestman escapes.

Nasty nippers

Some creepy crawlers have pincers at their tail end. In some species these are harmless, but in others they can give a nasty nip.

Earwigs

There are about 1800 species of earwigs, and at least one of them probably lives in your garden. Earwigs are mainly nocturnal. During the day, they hide in dark cracks and under stones. At night, they hunt for other insects, plants, and ripe fruit. Some earwigs use their nippers to hold on to prey or to grip their mate when mating.

Hellgrammites

Hellgrammites are the larvae of dobsonflies. They hide under rocks in fast-flowing streams and wait for prey to pass. Then they pounce. When the larvae are 2 to 3 years old, they crawl out of the water and burrow into damp soil. Two weeks later, they emerge as adult dobsonflies, and only live for about two more weeks.

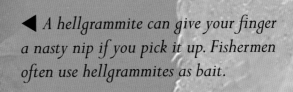

◀ *A hellgrammite can give your finger a nasty nip if you pick it up. Fishermen often use hellgrammites as bait.*

Long ago, people believed that earwigs crawled inside the ears of people as they slept, and burrowed into their brains.

▲ *Many species of earwig have nippers that look fearsome, but are actually soft and cannot hurt humans. Earwigs can open and close their nippers like scissors.*

Diplurans

Diplurans look like tiny, pale earwigs. They have pincers at their tail end. To catch prey, a dipluran burrows into soft soil until only its pincers are above ground. If tiny creatures, such as springtails or insect larvae, pass by, the dipluran snatches them into its burrow and eats them. Some species eat only rotting plant material.

▶ *Diplurans do not have eyes. Instead they have light detectors to help them find their way about.*

Beastly beetles

The ancient Egyptians believed that scarabs, or dung beetles, kept the world revolving like a huge ball of dung, or **feces**. They worshiped the beetles and carved huge statues of them in some of their temples.

Dung beetles

Dung beetles live in many different **habitats**, including deserts, forests, and grasslands. They feed on the animal dung of plant-eating animals, such as rabbits, cattle, and elephants. Dung beetles squeeze and suck liquid out of the manure.

▼ *Using their back legs, some dung beetles roll animal dung into balls larger than themselves, and use these balls as a supply of food.*

Burying beetles

Burying beetles bury dead creatures, such as birds or mice, in a hole in the soil. They strip the feathers or fur from the dead creature and line the hole with the material. The female lays her eggs in the soil around the hole. When the eggs hatch, the larvae move into the dead body to feed.

◀ *Burying beetles use their antennae to detect dead animals, such as this slug, from a long way off.*

Foul fact!

Some burying beetles regurgitate the flesh of dead creatures to feed their young.

Stag beetles

Stag beetle larvae live for several years, eating rotting wood. They can be found in the woodlands of southern and central Europe, and also in parks and gardens that have tree stumps or logs. The larvae change, or **metamorphose**, into beetles. In summer, the beetles fly about, rather clumsily, in search of mates.

▶ *Male stag beetles have enormous jaws that resemble a stag's antlers. They use them to fight rival males for the best mating sites.*

Horrid guests

Creepy crawlers are at their creepiest when they share our homes. They appear to watch us from cracks in the wall, or scuttle out from under furniture and make us jump.

▲ *Flour mites may infest fresh bread or flour if it is not kept in a cool, dry place.*

Flour mites

Flour mites are tiny creatures that live in and feed off flour, grains, and seeds. A female flour mite can lay 500 to 800 eggs in her lifetime. Flour infested with mites smells sweet and sickly. If you want to test whether there are mites in your flour, sprinkle some on a flat surface and look at it through a magnifying glass. The flour will become bumpy and uneven, and a tiny creature may emerge.

Silverfish

The silverfish has existed for over 300 million years. It eats the **starch** and sugars found in glue, book bindings, textiles, and even the dandruff that falls from our heads. However, it can survive for a year without eating.

◄ *The silverfish prefers to live in warm, damp places, such as bathrooms or underneath floors. It can run extremely fast.*

Cockroaches

About 25 to 30 cockroach species are regarded as pests. They can carry serious diseases, including **dysentery** and **typhoid**. Cockroaches live all around the world. Some species prefer kitchens and laundries, which get hot and steamy, while others live in forests. They live in groups, hiding by day in dark corners and coming out at night. Some species feed on people's leftover food and garbage.

▶ *There may be as many as 7500 species of cockroaches. Some types of cockroach can survive for a month without food, and can last without air for 45 minutes.*

Foul fact!

A cockroach's feces contain chemicals that other cockroaches sniff to find food and water.

21

Creepy disguise

Many creepy crawlers are camouflaged so they can hide. Some hide from predators, and others hide so they can catch prey.

▲ *The decorator crab* **camouflages** *itself all over so that predators find it hard to spot.*

▼ *The orchid mantis is a type of praying mantis. It has enlarged leg segments that resemble petals.*

Decorator crab

The decorator crab has small hooks on its back. It uses these to attach bits of seaweed or sponges to itself. The decorations act as camouflage. Sometimes the crab attaches to a sea anemone. Predators, such as small octopuses, are put off attacking, because sea anemones sting.

Flower mantids

Flower mantids are colored to look like the flowers on which they live. Their camouflage helps them to avoid predators and to catch prey. The mantids sit very still and wait for prey, such as flies, bees, butterflies, and moths, to come within reach. Then they pounce. The orchid mantis also eats tiny pieces of banana.

Foul fact!

The female Macleay's specter stick insect can curl her tail over her body like a scorpion.

▶ If threatened, the Macleay's specter stick insect sways like a dry leaf blowing in a breeze.

Macleay's specter stick insect

The Macleay's specter stick insect, or giant prickly stick insect, lives in New Guinea and northern Australia. A female can lay thousands of eggs in her lifetime. The eggs can take up to two years to hatch. The newly hatched young, called **nymphs**, resemble ants.

Pond perils

There are many strange creatures living in ponds, streams, and rivers around the world. Some of these **aquatic** creepy crawlers have fierce eating habits.

▶ *Giant water bugs live in ponds and streams in North America, South America, and East Asia.*

▼ *A dragonfly larva has hooks on its hinged jaw. It shoots out its lower jaw and stabs its prey with the hooks. Then it tugs the prey back into its mouth.*

Giant water bugs

Giant water bugs prey on small fish, frogs, and salamanders. They stab their prey with their sharp "beak" and inject their saliva into the prey's body. The saliva contains **enzymes** that make the prey's body dissolve, and the bugs suck up the liquid.

Dragonfly larvae

Dragonfly larvae are aggressive underwater predators. They have large eyes, which they use to spot their prey—water bugs, tadpoles, and even small fish. The larvae propel themselves through the water by forcing a current of water out of their rear end.

◄ *Water scorpions are so-called because their front legs look a little like a scorpion's pincers.*

Water scorpions

Water scorpions are a kind of giant water bug. Some are long and thin, and are called needle bugs. Others have broad bodies. They lurk near the edges of ponds, preying on tadpoles and small fish, which they grasp with their front legs.

Foul fleas

Fleas are tiny creatures, but they cause a lot of trouble. Not only do they bite animals and people, making them itch horribly, but they also carry and spread diseases.

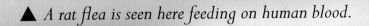

▲ *A rat flea is seen here feeding on human blood.*

▼ *The human flea also feeds on pigs. It is able to jump higher than the rat flea, as pigs are higher off the ground than rats.*

Rat flea

The rat flea is a carrier of **bubonic plague**, also known as the Black Death. It can pass this disease to humans. First the flea feeds on a rat that is carrying plague **bacteria**, and takes in the bacteria without being harmed. Then it feeds on a human, passing the bacteria into the person's blood. Bubonic plague is rare today, but over the centuries it has killed many hundreds of millions of people.

Human flea

The human flea is rare today, as it does not like the dry conditions created by central heating. But it used to be very common. In ancient China, flea traps made from ivory or bamboo were warmed and put into beds to catch the fleas. In 16th-century England, rich ladies wore fur collars known as "flea cravats" to catch the fleas, which were then shaken out.

Cat flea

The cat flea is the most common type of flea. It is found all over the world. Like other fleas, it feeds on fresh blood. The cat flea bites and sucks the blood of cats, dogs, and humans. The bites make small, red bumps on the skin that are extremely itchy. Fleas lay up to one egg an hour. The larvae that hatch develop into adults inside a silk **cocoon**.

▶ *Fleas can jump 150 times their own length. They jump to move from one host animal to another.*

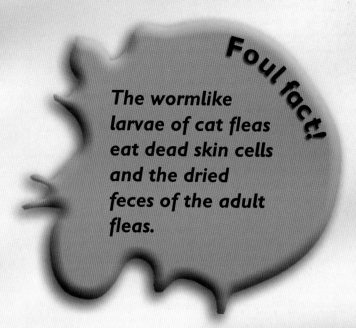

Foul fact!

The wormlike larvae of cat fleas eat dead skin cells and the dried feces of the adult fleas.

Make it!

Create your own creepy crawler and watch it scuttle away across the table.

1 Please ask an adult to do all of step 1. Slice off the last inch from the end of a candle and remove the wick. Enlarge the hole left by the wick by carefully scraping with a cocktail stick. Cut a groove across one end of the candle.

3 Poke the elastic band through the hole in the middle of the cotton reel. Push half a matchstick through the loop to keep the elastic band in place. Push another matchstick into one of the holes in the cotton reel to stop the half match stick from turning.

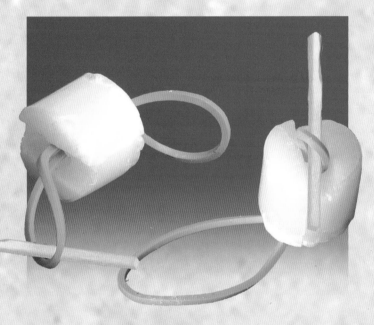

2 Push an elastic band through the piece of candle so it sticks out at both ends. Poke a matchstick through the end of the elastic band and fit it into the groove so that it stays in place.

4 Your cotton reel creepy crawly is now ready to decorate.

28

5 Cut out two strips of card or colored paper. Wind one strip around the cotton reel and stick it in place with glue. Wind the other strip around the candle and stick it in place. Decorate the card with glitter glue. You could make some wings from card and attach them as well.

6 Wind the elastic band by turning the matchstick "handle." Let go of the model and watch it "crawl" or roll away!

Glossary

Ambush
To attack something after lying in wait for it to approach or pass nearby.

Antennae
Long feelers on the heads of insects and crustaceans.

Aquatic
"Aqua" means water. Aquatic animals live in water.

Bacteria
Very small organisms that are found everywhere. Some bacteria cause illnesses, such as stomach upsets.

Bubonic plague
A serious, often fatal, disease caused by bacteria. The disease may be passed from rats to humans by fleas that have lived on infected rats. The illness causes fever, and dark bumps, called buboes, develop on parts of the body.

Camouflage
An animal that is camouflaged is difficult to spot because its patterns or colors blend in with the background.

Cocoon
A silky pouch spun by the larvae of many insects, such as silkworms and caterpillars. It covers the larva and keeps it safe as it develops into an adult.

Colony
A group of the same kind of animal living together. Insect colonies are usually organized so that every creature has a job to do within the colony.

Crustaceans
Creatures that are covered with a hard shell, such as lobsters, shrimps, crabs, and, on land, woodlice.

Dysentery
An infection, often caused by bacteria, that leads to severe diarrhea.

Enzymes
Natural chemicals. They help the bodies of creatures and humans to work properly.

Eyestalks
Movable stalks with an eye at their tip. They are found in crustaceans, such as crabs, and in some mollusks, such as snails.

Fangs
Long, sharp teeth. In a snake, fangs are often hollow and are used to inject venom into their prey.

Feces
Waste matter that is produced when an animal digests food. The feces of plant-eating animals are often called dung. Bird droppings are a mixture of feces combined with urine.

Fungi
Plants without leaves or flowers, such as yeasts, molds, mushrooms, and toadstools. Fungi grow on other plants or on decayed material.

Habitat
The natural surroundings where an animal lives. A desert habitat, for example, is dry and usually only a few types of plants grow in the sandy or stony ground.

Larvae

The newly hatched stage of a creature such as a butterfly. A butterfly's larva is a caterpillar. Larvae change to look quite different as adults.

Leaf litter

Dead plant material made from decaying leaves, twigs, and bark.

Metamorphose

When an animal goes through metamorphosis, it changes completely. A caterpillar changes into a butterfly or moth, and a tadpole changes into a frog.

Nocturnal

Animals that are nocturnal are active at night, when they move around and hunt for food. During the day, they rest and sleep.

Nymphs

The young or larval stage of some animals. Nymphs change into a different form as they become adults.

Predator

A creature that hunts and kills other animals for food.

Prehistoric

Belonging to very ancient times. Dinosaurs were alive in prehistoric times—the time before recorded history.

Prey

An animal that is hunted by another animal for food.

Rain forest

Dense tropical forests found in areas of very heavy rainfall.

Regurgitate

To bring food back into the mouth after it has been swallowed.

Reptile

Cold-blooded animals that have a backbone and short legs or no legs at all, such as snakes, lizards, and crocodiles.

Saliva

The liquid produced in the mouth to keep it moist and to help break down and swallow food.

Soldier termite

Every termite colony has a large number of soldier termites. They have large mandibles, or jaws, which they use to defend the colony against enemies, usually ants. Some termites also secrete toxic chemicals.

Species

A group of animals with similar characteristics to each other, and that can breed with each other.

Starch

A carbohydrate found in foods such as potatoes, bread, and pasta, but also found in paper, textiles, and glue.

Typhoid

A serious infectious disease caused by bacteria. It causes headaches, fever, and reddish spots all over the body, and can be fatal to humans.

Venom

The poison used by some mammals, snakes, and spiders to paralyze or kill their prey.

Worker termite

Within a termite colony the worker termite, which is often blind, is responsible for nest-building and the care of the young.

Index